WORLD*focus*

Pakistan

ELSPETH CLAYTON

Contents

Introduction

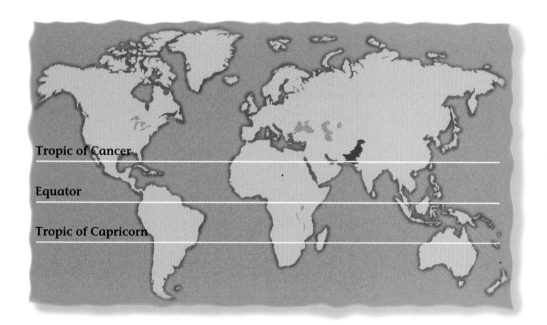

Tropic of Cancer

Equator

Tropic of Capricorn

Introduction

Pakistan is a country in south-west Asia. Its neighbours are Iran, Afghanistan, China and India. The River Indus rises in the north in Kashmir, and flows the whole length of the country to the Arabian Sea. This great river has given life to the people of Pakistan for the whole of its complex and colourful history.

People have been living in the area now called Pakistan for many thousands of years. There were great cities here before the cities of Mesopotamia and the tower of Babel, and long before the empires of Egypt, Greece and Rome.

Geography

Most of Pakistan is either mountainous or desert, and most of it is very dry. Only the Indus **river basin**, and the fertile **plains** of Punjab are lush and green. Unlike India and Bangladesh, only a few places in Pakistan benefit from the **monsoon** seasons. Three-quarters of the country gets less than 250 millimetres of rain a year. In comparison the UK gets, on average, 500 to 1000 millimetres of rain a year.

△ Where is Pakistan?

▷ Villages in southern Sindh bake in the sun all year round, but villages high in the mountains have freezing, snowy winters.

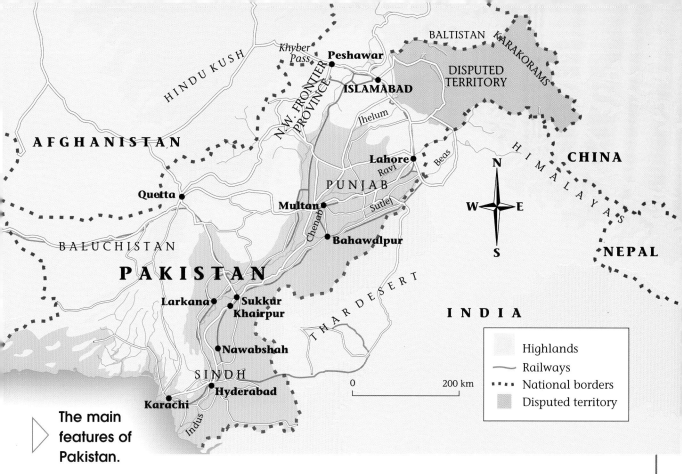

The main features of Pakistan.

Four mountain ranges meet in the north of Pakistan; they are the Karakorams, the Pamirs, the Himalayas and the Hindu Kush. Their mountains are some of the highest in the world, and have some of the longest **glaciers** in the world.

Climate

The hottest months of the year are June and July, when temperatures in the Indus plain and in parts of Baluchistan reach more than 50° C. But the average summer temperature is between 35 and 40° C. In the winter months, on the plain, the temperature falls to about 20° C, but in the northern valleys of Hunza and Baltistan it can be as low as minus 20° C.

3

The people

This area of Asia has seen many changes in its population – from the earliest **nomadic** peoples more than 10,000 years ago, to the first settled farmers living along the Indus. There have also been many invaders, from Cyrus the Great of Persia, Alexander the Great of Greece, and the British in the last century. People still move to Pakistan today. This time they are not invaders, but **refugees** from the civil war in Afghanistan looking for a safe place to stay.

A mixture of peoples

All of these events and peoples have come together over the centuries to make the culture and traditions of Pakistan. Together they created the stories, poems, songs, music and dances enjoyed in Pakistan today.

△ During the civil war in Afghanistan, about 4 million refugees fled to Pakistan.

The official language of Pakistan is Urdu – but other major languages are spoken. These are Punjabi, Sindhi, Pushto, Baluchi, Seraiki, Hindko and Brahui. Although there are many different ethnic groups in Pakistan, more than 95 per cent of all Pakistanis are Muslims and Islam is the country's official religion. There are also some Hindus and Christians, and a few Parsees.

Making Pakistan

Before 1947, when the British ruled the area which is now divided into Pakistan, India and Bangladesh, Muslims and Hindus alike dreamt of independence. When the British left, the Muslims were granted their own homeland – Pakistan.

▷ Ashraf is from the Sheedi community, thought to be descended from Africans shipwrecked on the coast long ago.

▽ Some Muslim women wear a flowing burqa whenever they leave their house. Others wear a dupatta, a scarf covering their head and shoulders.

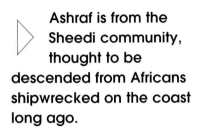

Originally Pakistan was in two bits, a thousand miles apart, on either side of India, called East and West Pakistan. They were ruled as one country by one government, but the people from each part spoke a different language, and had a different way of life, even though they were all Muslims. They wanted to run their own lives, and be able to speak their own language. In 1971 a civil war broke out between the two Pakistans. East Pakistan became a separate country called Bangladesh, and West Pakistan became known simply as Pakistan.

Where do people live?

Around 130 million people live in Pakistan. About one third of them live in towns and cities, the rest live in the countryside. Pakistan is made up of four provinces: Sindh, Punjab, North-West Frontier Province, and Baluchistan.

Sindh

Sindh province is named after the River Indus. The fertile **plains** of Sindh have been farmed for nearly 5000 years. Today, looking at the neat fields and villages it is hard to believe that Sindh was once covered with forests inhabited by wild animals such as tigers and elephants. Away from the river and fields are the sand dunes of the Thar Desert. Sindh's capital city, Karachi, is the centre of finance and business for the whole of Pakistan.

▽ Islamabad, the capital city of Pakistan. It is only 30 years old and some parts are still being built.

Punjab

The name Punjab means five rivers. They are the Sutlej, Beas, Ravi, Chenab and Jhelum which all flow into the Indus. Punjab is home to 56 million people, that is more than half of all the people living in Pakistan. The rivers have made Punjab the most fertile area of Pakistan. There is a lot of industry here too. Just as in Sindh, away from the rivers the land is desert where few people live. The capital of Punjab is Lahore, which is probably Pakistan's most famous town.

 Villages like Sunaki, in Punjab, look very pretty surrounded with lush green fields.

North-West Frontier Province (NWFP)

The word khaki (which means 'dust-coloured') comes from here, and that is the colour of much of this rugged province. But there are also fertile valleys where all sorts of crops can be grown. Peshawar is the capital of NWFP, and lies at the Pakistan end of the famous Khyber Pass. No one knows how old the city is, but some of the most famous travellers in history have been to Peshawar, including Alexander the Great and Marco Polo. Between 3 and 4 million Afghan **refugees** found shelter in NWFP.

Baluchistan

Baluchistan is mountainous and very dry and barren. Although it is the largest province, only 4 million people live here, fewer than live in the city of Karachi, and there are few big towns here besides the province's capital, Quetta. The mountains of Baluchistan are cut by 'passes', narrow passages which everyone who travels overland to Pakistan must find their way through. Because of Baluchistan's position, it has also been a home for many thousands of refugees from Afghanistan.

Agriculture

To grow anything you need water, and away from the rivers and **irrigation** systems, there are many areas in Pakistan where very little grows.

In Baluchistan and the Thar Desert, where there is not enough rainfall to grow crops, many families keep livestock (cattle, sheep and goats) which graze the sparse vegetation. These families are called **pastoralists**. In Baluchistan, the pastoralists are also **nomads** – taking their flocks from place to place looking for grazing land and water, and escaping from the extremes of temperature.

The granary of India

In Punjab, with its five rivers and network of canals, there is plenty of water for growing crops. Throughout the centuries, Punjab has always been the most fertile and richest province in the country, and was once called 'the granary of India' because it produced so much grain. Here, on thousands of small farms, people grow wheat, rice, sugar, fruit, tobacco, cotton, and many varieties of vegetables. Punjab mangoes are famous throughout Pakistan.

Farmers

People have been farming in Sindh for nearly 5000 years. Unlike Punjab, much of the land here is owned by big landowners, and is farmed by tenant farmers or **sharecroppers**. Sharecroppers do not own land, but give part of the harvest to the landowner as rent. Irrigation is even more important here than in Punjab.

Sugar cane is an important crop for farmers in Sindh.

Thousands of kilometres of canals and water courses irrigate more than 16 million hectares of land. Grain and cotton are grown, but Sindh is best known for producing high-quality fruit – mangoes, guavas and citrus fruits, and the best bananas in Pakistan.

Orchards
The fertile valleys of NWFP are also famous for fruit, but this time for apples, peaches, apricots, mulberries, cherries, lemons, oranges, lychees, and strawberries, and also for almonds and walnuts. Farmers there grow wheat, maize and rice, and all sorts of vegetables.

Market traders sell many fresh fruits and vegetables all grown in Pakistan. How many can you name?

Fishing
In villages along the rivers and coast, fishing is an important source of food and income. Usually men catch fish, but in the Punjab village of Chak Ghulam Mohammed women and girls also row boats and fish using nets. This is very unusual, and they have persuaded their village to build a fish pond, so that they can make more money for the village.

A growing problem

In some parts of Sindh, farmers cannot grow crops without **irrigation**, but over the years so much irrigation has been used that the ground has become **waterlogged**, and the soil is **saline**. Soil becomes saline when water stays in the soil and makes the salts deep in the soil dissolve and rise to the surface.

Not many plants like growing in salty soil with too much water, and they die. That is as bad as not having enough water, and more difficult to put right.

The problem in Pabban

In the villages around Pabban, near Hyderabad in central Sindh, very heavy rainfall and floods in 1992 made the problem even worse. Now the orchards of mango trees are dying, and crop yields are falling. Fertile fields are turning to wasteland. A group of villagers is trying to solve this serious problem.

▽ Ahmad Khan grows trees to sell to local farmers.

First, members of the group did a survey of the whole area to find out how many farmers were having problems. Then they installed special instruments called **piezometers** to measure the **water table**. They found that in some places the water is only 22.5 cm below ground, meaning that the water table has risen by more than 60 cm in two years.

Finding answers

One answer is to use irrigation water more carefully, so the group has installed new control points along the canal to stop farmers taking too much water. Another answer is to plant crops that can cope with saline and waterlogged soil.

△ Baksh Khan is measuring the depth of the water table.

They have discovered that some trees, including poplar and eucalyptus, will soak up the water. Some farmers are experimenting and planting them around their land so that they can dry up the soil. When the trees are big enough they can be cut down and sold to the paper-mills, so they will help to earn money too.

Where they can, the group has helped less well-off farmers to plant new orchards. This time, as well as planting new mango trees, they are planting guava and chikoo, which are able to grow in wetter soil.

Most important of all, the group is working together with the farmers to put things right again.

Industry

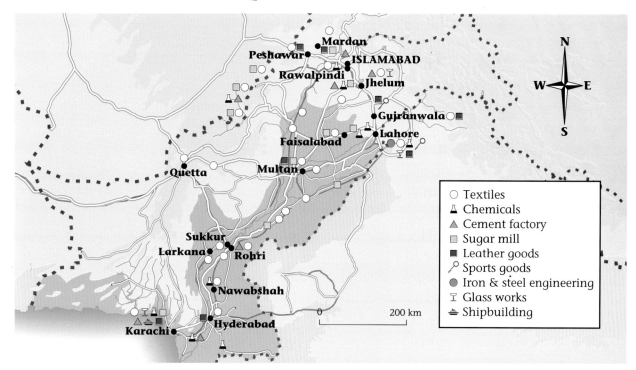

Legend:
- ○ Textiles
- ⚗ Chemicals
- ▲ Cement factory
- ▢ Sugar mill
- ■ Leather goods
- ⚲ Sports goods
- ● Iron & steel engineering
- ♆ Glass works
- ⚓ Shipbuilding

0   200 km

Look at the map, and you will see that most of the industries in Pakistan are in Punjab, and almost all of them are along the rivers. Some of the industries use the river for transport and most of them need water for their processes. Some also discharge chemicals and waste products into the rivers. In Punjab they make everything from bolts to zips, as well as fabrics and chemicals, and some of them process agricultural crops, such as cotton and sugar cane.

But there is one industry that you won't see marked on the map; wherever you go, around every town and city you see the tall, smoking chimneys of the **bhattas** (brick kilns). The bhattas are one of the biggest sources of work outside agriculture in Pakistan.

Life at Nasir Bhatta

Nasir Bhatta, near Lahore in Punjab, is owned by Mohammed Nasir Hussain. 'I own 34.5 hectares of land. On it there's the kiln, 40 houses for the labourers, and a school. The kiln is in operation for ten months of the year, and closed for the two months of the monsoon.'

△ Most of Pakistan's industries are in Punjab.

▷ Razia helps to make bricks, putting clay into a mould, then turning it out to dry.

Families are paid by the number of bricks they make a day, so the more of you working the more bricks you can make. The average number of bricks a family makes is 1000 a day.

Razia's day

Razia is nine years old. She and her family – her mother, grandmother and three younger brothers and sisters – live and work at Nasir Bhatta. After doing the housework, Razia goes to school for two hours in the morning. Then she goes to the brick field and works with her mother. Razia's father died a year ago, so they have to work even harder to make their 1000 bricks every day. When her mother isn't well, Razia doesn't go to school at all, and spends all day making bricks on her own.

How to make a brick

● First you mix the clay, making sure that there aren't any stones in it.

● Put the clay in the mould.

● Turn it out carefully.

● Dry it in the sun, turning it so that each side dries evenly.

● Bake it in a kiln.

Staying healthy

The healthier you are, the longer you are likely to live. People who do not have enough to eat, or are homeless, are said to be living in **poverty**. They will be ill more often than richer people, and they may not live as long. There are 35 million poor people in Pakistan – that is over a quarter of the population. People in Pakistan can expect to live only until they are 58. In the UK, we can expect to live 20 years longer.

Water for health

Clean water is important for good health. People who have a good water supply, such as a tap or pump in their house, can use as much water as they need for drinking and cooking, and for washing. If they have to collect water from a well or pump and carry it home to use, they will not use as much water.

▷ Water that stands in the fields provides a place for mosquitoes to breed, and spreads illness.

If they must pay for water to be delivered, then they will use even less. People also need efficient ways of dealing with sewage and dirty water because diseases such as cholera and typhoid are passed on through dirty and infected water. In Pakistan, only half the population have safe drinking water, and barely a quarter have good **sanitation**.

Malaria

One of the main causes of death in Pakistan is malaria, a fever passed on in mosquito bites. In Pabban and the nearby villages more people are getting malaria every year. The waterlogged and boggy soil, and the warm climate, are ideal conditions for mosquitoes to live and breed. Many people recover from malaria, but they may suffer from fever for years after.

Children

In Pakistan, 99 out of every 1000 babies die before their first birthday. After malaria, illnesses like measles, mumps and chicken pox are the second biggest cause of death. These are diseases which healthy children recover from without any problem. In Pakistan many poor children do not have enough to eat, and their bodies are too weak to fight the diseases.

◁ Drinking water that may be dirty or polluted makes people ill. Diseases like cholera and typhoid are spread by polluted water, but some families have no other choice.

Health care

When we are ill we all expect to be able to visit a doctor or hospital. In Pakistan there are health services – doctors and health centres – for only just over half of the population. Many people rely on health-workers who visit their village once or twice a week, and people may have to travel to the nearest town when they need to see a doctor.

Baqar Nizamani

PARAS

A Nazeer	**I** Hajam
B Niazo	**J** Meero Sheedi
C Shah	**K** Kham Kori
D Iqeal	**L** Jahoo Para
E Qasim Khaskhau	**M** Saraj
F Ghulam Rasool	**N** Molap Sheedi
G Mataro Khaskheli	**O** Nizamani plot
H Otaq	

Map legend:
- House
- Shop
- Masjid (Mosque)
- Bus stop
- Tent
- Khad = Low-lying area where water collects

In Sindh province, about 10 kilometres along the road from Hala to Shahdadpur is the village of Baqar Nizamani. There's not much to see from the road, just a couple of teashops, a **mosque**, a bus stop, and a few stalls which include a bicycle repairer and a tailor. Most of the village is hidden behind the trees, up a winding lane.

Family homes

You can't see much more even when you are in the middle of the village! All the houses are tucked away behind high walls or thick thorn hedges. About 1000 people live in the village, which is divided into family groups called **paras**.

△ The village of Baqar Nizamani.

Living off the land

Between the village and the road are fields of wheat and banana plants. This area of Sindh grows the best bananas in Pakistan, and lorries come to collect them for delivery all over the country. As well as wheat and bananas, people here grow cotton, sugar cane and onions to sell, and lots of other vegetables, such as potatoes, tomatoes and cauliflowers, to eat themselves.

Most people in the village make a living from the land. Some own their own land, and others work as labourers helping with the ploughing, weeding and harvesting. In the village there are also tailors, mechanics, a blacksmith, two flour mills, and teashops where the men meet to talk or play cards after work.

Nearby towns

When the villagers want to go shopping they travel by bus into the nearby towns of Hala or Shahdadpur where there are large markets. Children who are old enough to go to college, travel every day into Hala, or stay in a college hostel and come home at the weekends.

△ The streets of the village are always busy.

Village life

Life in Baqar Nizamani is much like life in your community. People work, go to school or college, eat, sleep, play, celebrate festivals and weddings, go to the cinema and watch television.

Village houses

The houses here are designed to suit the **climate**. It is so hot that people spend most of the day inside, and the evening and sometimes the night, outside. Each house is built around a courtyard. The living area is along one side and is made up of one or two rooms used for storing clothes and household goods, and for sleeping in in the cool weather or when it rains. Sometimes the roof of the rooms is so wide, it provides shade in the courtyard for people to sit under.

▽ Half the families in Baqar Nizamani use the village well because they do not have a pump or well at home.

The kitchen is usually a separate room because most families cook on wood fires and they don't want everything to get smoky, and because it is so hot in the summer they want to keep the living area as cool as possible. About half the houses in the village have their own water pump, the rest get their water from an open well.

Women's work

The village women always have lots to do. People buy very little processed food, so wheat must be ground to make flour, milk churned into butter and spices ground for each meal. When the family needs new clothes, they buy cloth and take it to a tailor to be made up into the suits of baggy trousers called **shalwar** and long, loose tops called **kameez** or **kurta** which are worn by everyone. Each area of Pakistan has its own particular way of making and decorating clothes to be worn on special occasions.

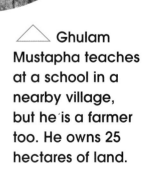

△ Ghulam Mustapha teaches at a school in a nearby village, but he is a farmer too. He owns 25 hectares of land.

Going to school

Baqar Nizamani has four schools, two for boys and two for girls. It is still quite unusual for girls from the village to go to secondary school and college, but things are changing as people understand that if girls and women are educated, they can make life better for their families and their community.

A day with Tariq

In the evenings Nuzhat, Tariq's mother, helps some of the village girls to read and learn the Qur'an.

Here is Tariq (standing) with his friends Mujib, Sikander and Imdad.

'My name is Tariq Nizamani. I live with my mother, my uncle and his wife and children, and my Aunt Nur. Our house is in the Nizamani Para. My uncle is a teacher at a school in another village, and my mother works at the girls' school here.'

Tariq at school

I am in the seventh grade at the boys' school near the Rohri Canal. We speak Sindhi at home, but at school I am learning Urdu and English, which is my favourite subject. My favourite lesson this week was a poem about a Neem Tree, because I love poetry, and it was a good story.

On school-days I get up between 6.30 and 7 a.m. I get dressed and have breakfast, and go off to school. I usually pack my school bag the night before so that it's all ready. I get home at about 2 p.m., have some lunch, and then have a rest till about 4 p.m.

After school

I go to the shops almost every day – there's usually something we need. Then I go out to play cricket with my mates. We play every day. At around 6 p.m. I go and sweep the yard and splash water on the ground to settle the dust and cool the atmosphere. That is called **chirkao**. After I've done that, I come home and watch television for a while, then I do my homework, eat, and go to bed at about 10 p.m.

△ Mr Fakhr sells everything from bubblegum to light bulbs in his shop.

Helping the community

On Fridays I go to the **mosque** to pray. My Uncle Akhter is a member of the village men's group, and sometimes I go and help them in the library they have built. It's still quite new, so there's always work to do numbering the new books, and keeping it tidy.

When I'm grown up I really want to be a pilot. But I don't want to leave Baqar Nizamani. I'll always live here, and I'll try to do the best I can for myself – and for the village.

Spare time

Everyone works hard in Pakistan – many people get up before dawn to start their long day's work and may not get home until sunset. All the shops and markets are closed on Fridays, which is the Muslim day of rest, like our Sunday. In towns and cities, office workers have Saturday off too, which is their chance to go to hockey or cricket matches, or to one of the many colourful markets or **bazaars** where you can find everything you could possibly need – food, jewellery, furniture, animals, shoes, carpets and flowers.

Sightseeing

Many people in Pakistan visit the tombs and shrines of Muslim saints and great spiritual leaders, and the sites of the ancient cities, such as Taxila and Mohenjodaro. The Moghul emperors and kings who once ruled over India and Pakistan left great fortresses, and beautiful palaces, tombs and gardens, which are also popular.

▽ Going to the cinema is very popular in Pakistan.

 Television is popular everywhere in Pakistan. Fifty families in Baqar Nizamani have TV sets. Some also have satellite TV.

Celebrations

Melas are great occasions with circuses, fairs, dancing, poetry and music. Some of them mark the different seasons of the year – in northern Pakistan, every town and village celebrates the coming of spring in March. In the city of Lahore everyone celebrates **Basant**, the start of spring, by flying colourful kites.

Religion

An important building in every village, town and city is the mosque. Muslim men and boys go there to pray at least once a week, on Fridays. There are many important Muslim festivals; one of them is at the end of Ramadan – a month of **fasting**. During Ramadan, no food is cooked or eaten between sunrise and sunset. At the end of 30 days there is a festival, Eid-ul-Fitr, which is a great celebration. Money is given to the poor, men go to the mosque to pray, and families and friends get together.

Journeys and transport

When you look at an atlas, and see Pakistan next to India, it looks quite small. But Pakistan covers over 796 square kilometres, which makes it more than three times bigger than the UK. Cars are very expensive in Pakistan, and not many people can afford them, so there are all sorts of other ways of getting about.

Around the village

Baqar Nizamani is small enough to walk around, but if you want to go to the next village, you could go by **tonga**, a horse-drawn buggy with seats, or scooter-rickshaw, a three-wheeler built around a motor-scooter which can carry two or three people. For longer journeys, such as to Hala, you catch the bus or minibus at the stop on the main road. It costs 30 rupees (that's about 63p) for a return ticket, which makes it quite expensive if you go to work or college every day.

△ Donkey carts are very useful but for longer journeys, people often use camel carts.

Long journeys

For even longer journeys, coaches and trains are popular. Pakistan has a good railway system which goes through every major town. Travelling by train can be exciting because there are huge rivers and very difficult terrain to cross – especially in the mountains! And although Pakistan has some very modern diesel trains, you can still see old steam trains puffing along.

Almost every city in Pakistan has an airport. It is a much quicker way to travel, and some journeys are so difficult by road, that the government pays most of the costs so that people can afford it.

Transporting goods

If you have goods to transport over short distances, you can use a donkey cart, a camel cart, or a tractor and trailer. But for longer journeys you can use the most colourful trucks in the world.

Truck owners in Pakistan decorate every bit of their vehicles, with anything from patterns and landscapes, to film stars, pop singers and politicians, and even religious sayings. The more beautiful the truck, it is said, the more careful the driver will be, and the safer your goods will be!

▽ The decorated lorries seen in Pakistan are famous world-wide.

Challenges

▽ The girls who live in Baqar Nizamani are lucky, and can go to school, even college if they want. In other areas, girls, especially from poor families, may only go to primary school.

Pakistan has made great progress since independence and its agricultural and other industries are flourishing. Many people have lives very similar to ours – they are able to buy all the things they need, have enough to eat, can pay for doctors and medicines, school and college. Some have holidays, and cars. But nearly 37 million people in Pakistan live in such poverty that they can't even buy enough food.

Women

Life is especially hard for poor women. In rural areas, women have a double workload. As well as all their

work at home, they also do a lot of agricultural work, especially at harvest time. They may also have to look after animals – such as sheep or goats – and have to collect water and firewood. Few girls from poor families go to school after the age of ten, and even fewer go to college, as they are needed to work. Life is very different for girls from wealthier familes; they can go to school, college and university, and can easily find work in offices, or as teachers, doctors and nurses.

Bonded labour

Bonded labour can be a form of slavery, and is very common in the **bhattas** (brick kilns). The workers are paid very low wages, so in order to live, they must borrow money from their employer.

△ Bonded labour is most common in the brick kilns. Labourers are in debt to their employer, and have to accept whatever they are paid, no matter how little.

This means that they are always in debt, and are forced to accept low wages and poor working conditions. When the work at one kiln is finished their debt is 'sold' by their employer to the next kiln boss.

Child labour

Many children have to work to help support their family. They work in the kilns or weave carpets, or in other small factories and industries. They often have to work long hours, are paid low wages, and work in very poor conditions. They have little chance to go to school, or even to play.

Fighting poverty

All through Pakistan there are groups of people working to make life better. Some are large organizations which work throughout the country fighting injustices like bonded labour, or to make working conditions for children better. It is very difficult for poor people to borrow money from banks, so some communities and groups start their own. Each person saves money every week or month, and then they can borrow more money when they need it. When they repay their loan they pay back a small amount extra. These are the sorts of groups that charities like Oxfam works with, supporting their efforts with money, advice, or training.

Looking at Pakistan

This book has only been able to show you a very little about life in Pakistan. Pakistanis describe their country as diverse. It means that it is a country of different peoples, languages, religions, customs and traditions, and ways of living.

The country looks different from place to place, and the weather is different, too – it can be raining and cold in Peshawar, while Karachi has a heatwave! Some areas are cold in winter and hot in summer, while others are hot in winter and even hotter in the summer! Everywhere you go the houses are different, too. Some are designed to stay warm in winter, others to stay cool all year round. And although almost everyone wears the **shalwar** and **kameez** or **kurta**, they are of different styles and designs and materials.

△ In Southern Sindh, the houses in Haji Sukio village are built to make the most of any breezes.

◁ Boys from Lahore, dancing at a local festival.

28

A child carpet weaver. Some people think we shouldn't buy carpets made by children.

The busy streets in towns and cities.

There are areas of wide pleasant roads of large houses for wealthy families, and areas of narrow lanes of small, crowded houses for poor families. There are bazaars and markets and modern shopping malls, and buffalo carts and aeroplanes.

Pakistan is one of the most prosperous countries in South-west Asia. The Pakistanis have achieved this through hard work, and by developing some of the industries the country needed. Some people have become very rich indeed – but many families are still very poor.

Glossary

Basant This holiday marks the beginning of spring. Everyone goes outside, or onto the flat roofs of their homes, and flies kites.

Bazaar Another name for a market.

Bhatta A brick kiln.

Chirkao After you sweep the ground, you sprinkle water on it, to keep the dust down and cool the air. This is known as chirkao.

Debt repayments Sometimes governments borrow money from international banks or other governments and must repay the money. The money they owe is called a debt.

Fasting To go without food for a period of time. Often for religious reasons.

Glaciers Very slow moving rivers of ice found in high mountain ranges.

Irrigation In areas where there is not enough rainfall to grow crops, people dig canals and channels to take water from rivers or reservoirs to the fields where it is needed.

Kameez/kurta A long, loose top, worn over **shalwar**.

Mela A festival or exhibition.

Monsoon A seasonal wind which occurs in South-east Asia. The word is usually used to describe the wet weather brought by the summer winds which travel over the Indian Ocean to parts of India and Bangladesh.

Nomads People who do not live in one place, but travel from place to place with the seasons. They may have a home area which they return to from time to time. Sometimes, just the men and boys are nomads – taking flocks of animals in search of pasture – while the women, girls and old people stay at home.

Paras A family group which lives together. A para usually consists of parents and sons, and the sons' wives and children.

Pastoralists People who depend on animals – cattle, camels, donkeys, goats, sheep – for their living.

Piezometer What you use to measure the **water table**.

Plains Flat or gently rolling land. Plains quite often flood in the rainy season.

Qur'an The sacred book of Islam.

Refugees People who have had to leave their homes or country because of war, persecution or natural disaster.

River basin This is an area drained by a river and its tributaries.

Saline Water that is salty is called saline.

Sanitation The supply of clean water to homes and the removal of sewage and dirty water from homes.

Shalwar Baggy trousers.

Sharecroppers People who farm land belonging to someone else, and pay rent with part of their harvest.

Tonga A horse-drawn buggy with seats.

Water table The level at which you will find water if you dig a hole, like a well.

Waterlogged Land which is full of water and unable to grow plants.

Index

About Oxfam in Pakistan

The international family of Oxfams works with poor people and their organizations in over 70 countries. Oxfam believes that all people have basic rights: to earn a living, and to have food, shelter, health care, and education. Oxfam provides relief in emergencies, and gives long-term support to people struggling to build a better life for themselves and their families.

Oxfam UK and Ireland works in Pakistan to combat environmental problems, funding irrigation and other measures to prevent soil water-logging. Oxfam also helps provide adult education. With disabled people – particularly children – Oxfam supports groups offering special education, treatment and training. All of Oxfam's programme in Pakistan seeks to include and help women, who are often the most disadvantaged of the poor.

The publishers would like to thank the following for their help in preparing this book: Pramod Unia from the Oxfam Pakistan Desk; Yameema Mitha, Maryam Iqbal, Nuzhat Abbas, Imtiaz Pirzada, and the staff of the Oxfam Islamabad and Hyderabad offices for their help in organizing, translating, and travelling; the people of Baqar Nizamani and Pabban; the Oxfam photo library.

The Oxfam Education Catalogue lists a range of other resources on economically developing countries, including Pakistan, and issues of development. These materials are produced by Oxfam, by other agencies, and by Development Education Centres. For a copy of the catalogue contact Oxfam, 274 Banbury Road, Oxford OX2 7DZ, phone (01865) 311311, or your national Oxfam office.

Photographic acknowledgements
The author and publishers wish to acknowledge, with thanks, the following photographic sources:

All Oxfam copyright, by the following photographers: M. Semple pp3, 29*a*. P. Unia p4. M. Iqbal pp5, 11, 13, 14, 18, 20–21, 23, 27, 28*b*, 29. E. Clayton pp6, 7, 8, 9, 10, 15, 17, 19, 20, 21, 24, 26, 28*a*. R. Tallontire p22. P. McCulloch p25.

The publishers have made every effort to trace the copyright holders, but if they have inadvertently overlooked any, they will be pleased to make the necessary arrangement at the first opportunity.

Cover photograph: M. Iqbal

Note to the reader - In this book there are some words in the text which are printed in **bold** type. This shows that the word is listed in the glossary on page 30. The glossary gives a brief explanation of words which may be new to you.

First published in Great Britain by Heinemann Library, an imprint of Heinemann Publishers (Oxford) Ltd Halley Court, Jordan Hill, Oxford OX2 8EJ

OXFORD LONDON EDINBURGH MADRID ATHENS BOLOGNA PARIS MELBOURNE SYDNEY AUCKLAND SINGAPORE TOKYO IBADAN NAIROBI HARARE GABORONE PORTSMOUTH NH (USA)

© 1996 Heinemann Publishers (Oxford) Ltd.

00 99 98 97 96
10 9 8 7 6 5 4 3 2 1

British Library Cataloguing in Publication Data
Clayton, Elspeth
  Pakistan. – (Worldfocus Series)
  I. Title II. Series
  954.91

ISBN 0 431 07246 9 (Hardback)

ISBN 0 431 07241 8 (Paperback)

Designed and produced by Visual Image
Cover design by Threefold Design
Printed and bound in Britain by Bath Press Colourbooks, Glasgow

A 5% royalty on all copies of this book sold by Heinemann Publishers (Oxford) Ltd will be donated to Oxfam (United Kingdom and Ireland), a registered charity number 202918.

This book is to be returned on or before
the last date stamped below.

915·491

**Books are to be returned on or before
the last date below**

- 3 FEB 2000

1 6 APR 2002

2 3 SEP 2002

03 DEC 2002

17 AUG 2004

21 SEP 2004

LIBREX —